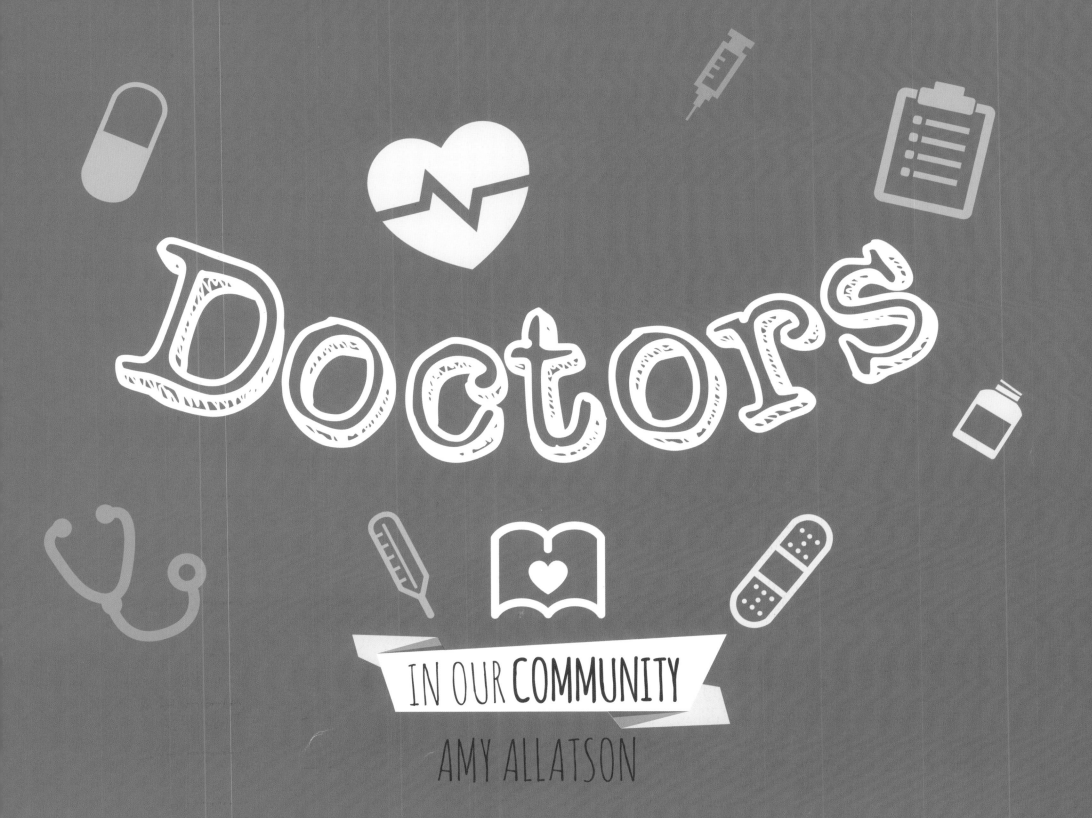

Doctors

IN OUR COMMUNITY

AMY ALLATSON

Contents

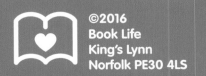

©2016
Book Life
King's Lynn
Norfolk PE30 4LS

ISBN: 978-1-910512-98-2

All rights reserved
Printed in Spain

Written by: Amy Allatson
Designed by: Drue Rintoul

A catalogue record for this book is available from the British Library.

What is a Community?

We all live together in a community. People in a community work together to help keep the local area clean and safe.

A TEACHER

There are many different people in a community, with many different jobs.
For example, a teacher helps us to learn at school.

What is a Doctor?

A doctor is a person that helps us to feel better when we are unwell.

A DOCTOR

Doctors work in a doctor's **surgery** or hospital. When people feel unwell they visit their local surgery or hospital.

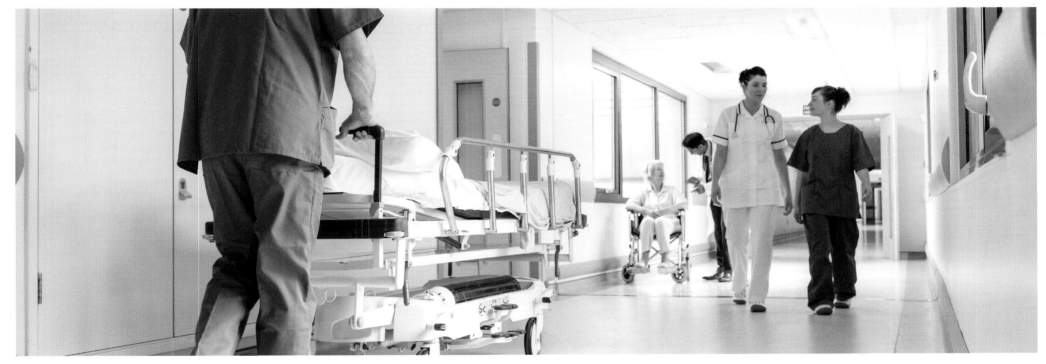

A HOSPITAL

How do Doctors Help Us?

We visit the surgery to find out why we are ill or injured. They treat **patients** with **medicines** and tell them what to do to feel better.

MEDICINES

Doctors can tell you how to live a healthy life. They tell you what food to eat and how much exercise you need to do.

EATING FRUIT HELPS US STAY HEALTHY.

When we have a sore throat, doctors use a special wooden stick to look into our mouths.

THEY ASK US TO SAY 'AHHHHH!'

STETHOSCOPE

They use a stethoscope to listen to our breathing: it tells them if there is something wrong with our chest.

Where do Doctors Work?

Doctors usually work in Surgeries. You can make an appointment at your local surgery to if you need to see a doctor.

Sometimes doctors work in buildings called hospitals. They are very big and you can usually see ambulances parked outside.

What do Doctors Use?

Doctors use many different pieces of **equipment**. A Stethoscope can be used to hear your heartbeat.

A STETHOSCOPE

A thermometer is used to measure our temperature. When your temperature is too high you are unwell.

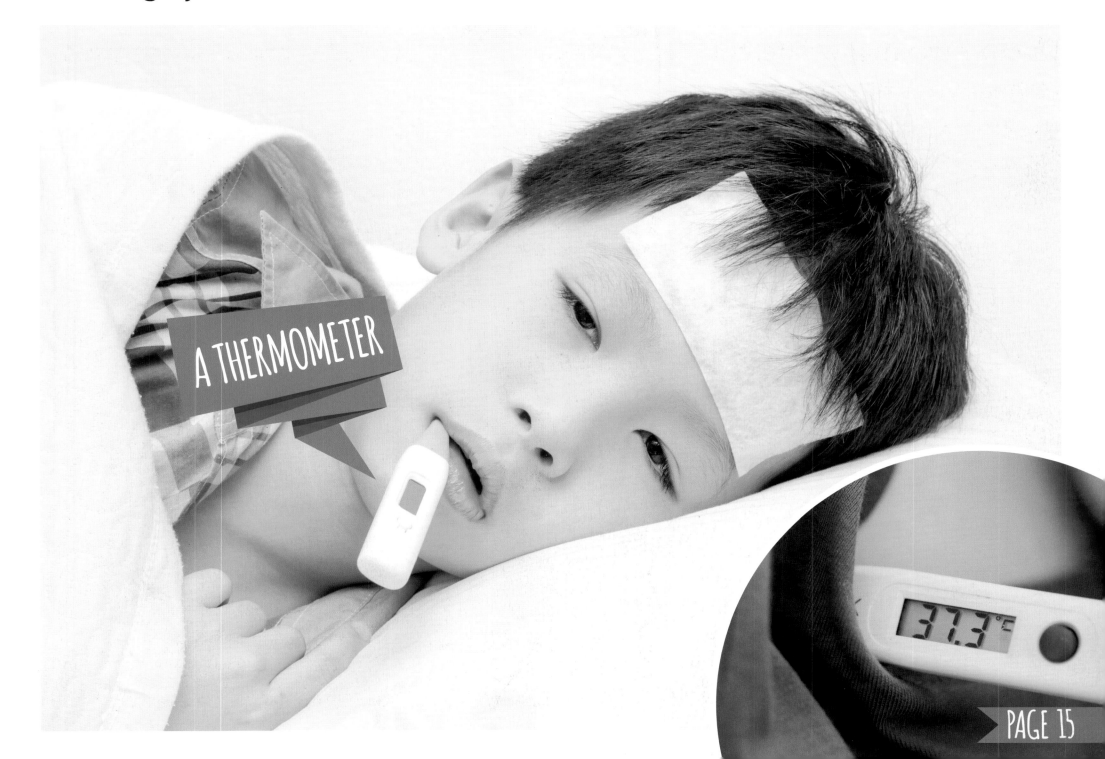

A THERMOMETER

What do Doctors Wear?

Doctors do not have to wear a **uniform** to work. They sometimes wear white coats and stethoscopes around their necks.

Doctors wear rubber gloves when they treat patients to keep them clean and safe.

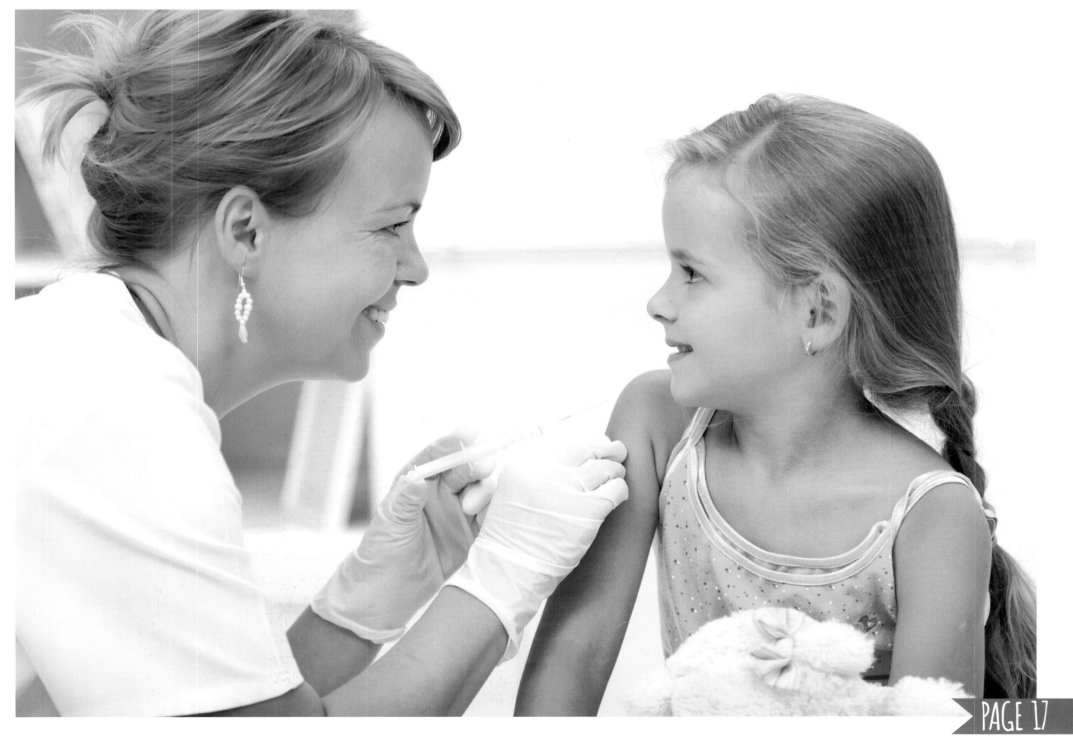

How do Doctors Travel?

If you are too ill to visit a doctor, they will visit you at home. They use a special doctor's car to travel around the community.

Doctors carry a doctor's bag with them. Carrying equipment with them, such as plasters, means they can help a patient straight away.

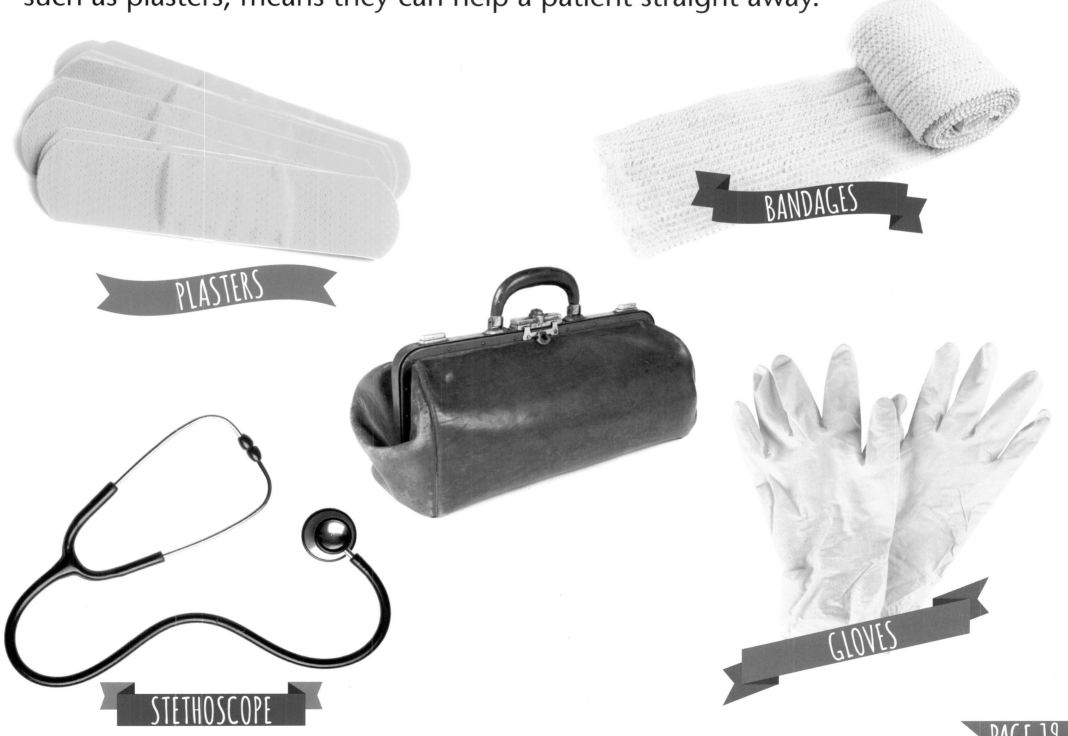

PLASTERS

BANDAGES

STETHOSCOPE

GLOVES

Visiting the Surgery

When you visit the Doctor's Surgery, you will speak to the **receptionist** who will let the doctor know you are there for your appointment.

You then wait in the waiting room for the doctor to see you.

WAITING ROOM

Can you Name...?

Can you name the equipment doctors use?
What do doctors use them for?

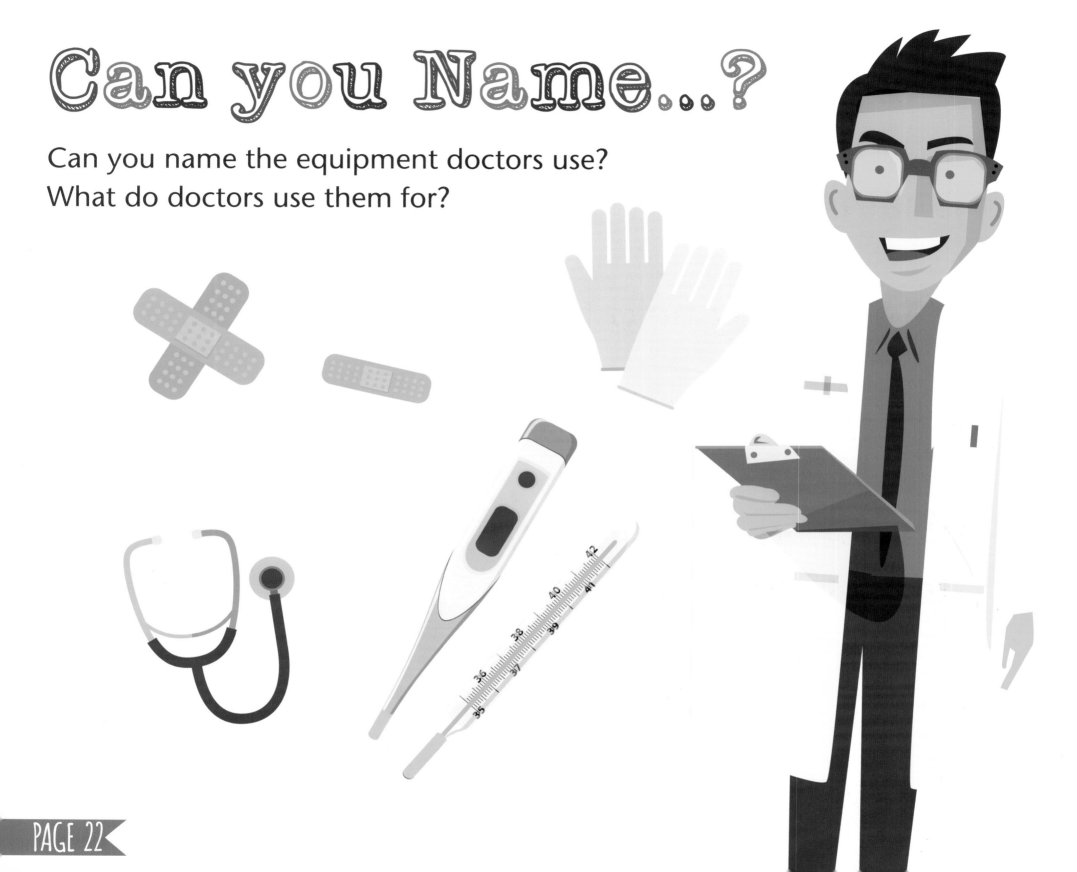

Quick Quiz

1. What is a doctor?

2. How do they help the community?

3. Where do doctors work?

4. What do doctors use stethoscopes for?

Index

Glossary

Community	A group of people who live in the same place.
Medicines	Liquids or pills that doctors give us, to make us feel better.
Receptionist	A person that helps to keep the doctor organised.
Surgery	A building where people visit the doctor.
Uniform	Clothes that show where you work or go to school.

Photocredits: Abbreviations: l-left, r-right, b-bottom, t-top, c-centre, m-middle. All images are courtesy of Shutterstock.com.
Front Cover - Aila Images, 2 - www.BillionPhotos.com, 3- Aila Images, 4 - Rawpixel, 5 - racorn, 6 - Aila Images, 7t - Spotmatik Ltd, 7b – Steve Design, 8bg – Monkey Business Images, 8inset - r.classen, 9top - airn, 9bottom - monticello, 10 - Ilike, 11 - Alexander Raths, 12br - Monkey Business Images, 12inset - spwidoff, 13bg - chrisdorney, 13inset - Lucian Milasan, 14bg - VGstockstudio, 14inset - IAKOBCHUK VIACHESLAV, 15bg - parinyabinsuk, 15inset - ikkker, 16 - michaeljung, 17 - Ilike, 18 JuliusKielaitis, 19: tl - Pamela D. Maxwell; tr - exopixel, m - Taborsky, bl - piotr_pabijan, br - Nataliya Kuznetsova, 20 - Robert Kneschke, 21 - Blend Images, 23 - IAKOBCHUK VIACHESLAV